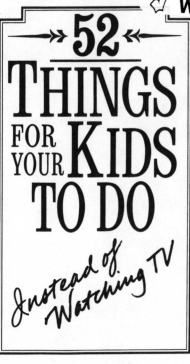

52
THINGS
FOR YOUR KIDS
TO DO
Instead of Watching TV

W9-BOX-984

≫ 52 ≪
THINGS
FOR YOUR KIDS
TO DO
Instead of Watching TV

Phil Phillips

OLIVER
NELSON

THOMAS NELSON PUBLISHERS
Nashville

Copyright © 1992 by Phil Phillips

All rights reserved. Written permission must be secured from the publisher to use or reproduce any part of this book, except for brief quotations in critical reviews or articles.

Published in Nashville, Tennessee, by Oliver-Nelson Books, a division of Thomas Nelson, Inc., Publishers, and distributed in Canada by Lawson Falle, Ltd., Cambridge, Ontario.

Unless otherwise noted, the Bible version used in this publication is THE NEW KING JAMES VERSION. Copyright © 1979, 1980, 1982, Thomas Nelson, Inc., Publishers.

Printed in the United States of America.

Library of Congress Cataloging-in-Publication Data
Phillips, Phil.
    52 things for your kids to do instead of watching TV / Phil Phillips.
        p.   cm.
    ISBN 0-8407-9638-2 (pbk.)
    1. Television and children—United States.   2. Creative activities and seat work.   3. Family recreation—United States.   I. Title.   II. Title: Fifty-two things for your kids to do instead of watching TV.
HQ784.T4P449   1992
302.23′45′083—dc20   92-14304
                                                                  CIP

1   2   3   4   5   6   —   97   96   95   94   93   92

To
our dear friends

Warren (Bear) and Jan Moseley

Thanks for pushing my wife
out into that aisle
—I'm forever indebted!

▲ Contents

▲ Introduction

Your children have a unique opportunity to spend close to fifteen thousand hours before the age of seven doing what they'll dream of being able to do the rest of their lives: playing.

Play is children's work. It is the way they explore the world.

Play is a state of mind—a view of the world that says, "I'm curious," "I want to know more," "I'd like to know why," and "I can have fun figuring out life and meeting new people and exploring new ideas."

Play is involvement with the world—sometimes with other children and sometimes with adults. It provides a means of learning how to cope with or conquer life's problems and how to converse, make decisions, and solve problems with life's co-travelers.

Play is the way children figure out how things work and what is most rewarding to them personally.

Much of what adults might call building, expressing, learning, experimenting, creating, or working is what children would call having fun or playing.

The greatest thief of playtime is television. It literally robs your children of experiences that will fashion their lives, expand their minds and hearts, and add layers upon layers of depth and character to their personalities. Stated another way, *the greatest enemy to their potential is television.*

What does television give to children in place of their creativity and energy? Prepackaged story lines. Commercials. A hefty dose of violence. An increasing number of occult messages. A skewed view of sexual relationships and the role of children in our society. And a lot of frenetic music accompanying a blur of meaningless motion programmed in such a way that children begin to see all of life in eight- to ten-minute time spans. Not only does television rob something precious from your children. It leaves a cheap, hollow substitute for real life in its place.

Your children will experience a better quality of life if you will limit their viewing of carefully selected television programs and videotapes to no more than four hours a week.

"But what can I encourage my kids to do instead of watch TV?" you may ask.

Here are 52 suggestions.

1 ▲ Reading

In the opinion of most parents I've asked, the number one preferred alternative activity to watching television for their children is reading.

Why Read?   Reading does several things far better than television:

- *Reading stimulates creativity.* Children must think the details of a scene or a character, even though a description may be provided by a book—thus envisioning clothing, facial gestures, sound of voice, surrounding environments, and action. What they envision is invariably far richer in detail and depth of characterization than are the images presented on most children's programs.
- *Reading stimulates problem-solving and decision-making skills.* Children learn how to develop reasoning ability as they read. The unfolding plot of a book invites the question, What do you think will happen next? For viewers of television, that ques-

tion is resolved too quickly to engage a response.

- *Reading allows children to absorb a story at their own pace.* Time-outs can be taken for daydreaming. The story can be picked up and put down at will. Children have control over the story—rather than the television set dictating the pace of action. Furthermore, they can reread a story as often as they like.

- *Reading helps children develop language ability.* Children learn new vocabulary words as they read. They encounter various patterns of sentence construction and the wonderful worlds of rhyme and alliteration. They learn the fine art of verbal jokes—puns and witticisms. They learn to distinguish characters by the words they speak rather than the way they look; they develop an understanding that people are more than their appearance. Children follow a line of reasoning far more clearly in print than on videotape. And in following a line of reasoning, they are learning to reason. Finally, children are given far more clues about a character's motivations and inner thought life and feelings in books than on TV.

- *Reading separates a story line from commercial messages.* The result is a seamless story, unpunctuated by product pitches. It follows that comprehension of the story is better when the story is read than when it is seen.

How to Choose? In choosing books for your children or in helping older children select books, consider these points:

1. Make certain the book is a challenge at, or slightly beyond, the individual's reading level. The book must not be too difficult to read, however. Children should be challenged to learn several new words with each book.

2. Make certain the book is in line with the values you are hoping to instill. A number of children's books promote occult practices and emphasize ghosts, goblins, monsters, and other fantasy creatures.

3. Some books are based on television programs or children's movies. In other cases, the books were classics first, and the media version followed. By letting your children read the book version of a popular story, you are helping them engage in a common experience with peers, yet without the extra doses of violence often included in the movie version.

Read Together Reading is an activity that unites parents and children. Read to your children. (Even older children will enjoy a book read by a parent for a few minutes a day.) Ask them to read to you. Make books a part of your conversations. Go to the library together each week. Build a library for your children of favorite, traditional, beautifully illustrated, and best-loved books. It will be a treasure they will value even more as the years go by.

2 ▲ "Make-Believe" Play

Encourage your children to make up story lines and to act out the plots they create:

- Make up characters.
- Give both voice and words to characters.
- Adopt mannerisms and costumes for the characters.
- Create sets or "stages" on which their characters might act out dramas.
- Engage in action sequences.

Exploration   Make-believe play isn't designed for performance or for review by adults (although the wise parent occasionally will unobtrusively watch kids at such play for signs of aggressive or inappropriate behavior). This play is simply for children's pleasure in exploring the world.

Children must be taught to play in this way. Sit down with them periodically and help them make up stories using toy props. Teach them how characters engage in dialogue. Give them ideas for a setting, such as a fort made from a card table, a roadway made from lined-up blocks, or an entire house contained in a bedroom or outlined in the dirt outside. Prime the pump of imagination.

Role-Play   Through make-believe play, children try on various roles in life. Suggest scenarios. For example, they might play "house" . . . "store" . . . "school" . . . "office" . . . "restaurant" . . . "church" (or synagogue) . . . "police station" . . . "fire station" . . . "Wild West fort" . . . "deserted island" . . . "space station" . . . "farm" . . . "ocean liner" . . . "hospital" . . . and so on. Imagination is the limit!

As they get older, encourage your children to try scenes from different time periods—colonial days, ancient times, or A.D. 2100. Encourage your children to play in a setting that might involve people of different races and cultures in a positive way. You may want to enhance the make-believe world with costumes and props in a "dress-up" trunk.

Cooperation   Group make-believe play helps children learn to play in a cooperative manner. Watch them as they play in small groups. Make suggestions that will allow (1) each child to have a turn as leader or plot creator—the child who sets the parameters of the action and scene, (2) each child to have a turn playing the leading character, whether hero or villain, (3) each child to have an opportunity to take part in the action (note: every child should have speaking lines), and (4) each child to have a say in how the play develops and is finally resolved. It takes practice to learn to play in a cooperative, fuss-free manner.

Back to Reality   All is reality to a child; some children have difficulty differentiating the fantasy world of their creation from the real world. Encourage make-believe play but continually call children back to reality when playtime is over.

3 ▲ Group Games and Sports

Send your children outside to play whenever possible. Provide sporting props and they will soon find that outside action play is more fun than watching sports on TV.

Various activities are appropriate for kids:

- Baseball or softball. Or kids can play catch without bats and bases.
- Soccer. It has rapidly become the sport of choice for children under ten.
- Basketball. If you don't have a hoop, your children can set up a trash can as a goal and even substitute a soccer ball for a basketball.
- Frisbee throwing. Your children may want to make up a Frisbee "golf course" or a Frisbee version of shuffleboard.
- Foursquare or twosquare. This bouncing ball game is popular on school playgrounds.
- Croquet. Kids can adapt a baseball bat and ball for play.
- Jump rope. Lots of different jumps and related rhymes and songs are possible.
- Marbles and jacks. These games can be played indoors, too.

Nerf balls, made of Nerf foam, are good for children from young ages to teens. Play with these items results in far fewer bruises and broken windows. Nerf sets for softball, field hockey, golf, Ping-Pong, and other sports can generally be used for indoor play as well as outdoor play.

With swing sets, tetherball courts, and other outdoor activity sets (which may include slides, rope ladders, and other climbing accessories), kids can burn up excess energy.

Add a net to the play action and you can create a variety of games and sports in your yard, on your driveway, or in your apartment house parking lot or patio area, such as tennis, volleyball, badminton, a soccerball version of Ping-Pong, and other games your children create.

Advantages Games and sports help children develop motor skills—both large muscle and small muscle—as well as hand-eye coordination. Children also learn the function of rules and concepts of fairness.

Encourage cooperative play rather than competitive play. Also encourage your children to let all playmates have a turn or be part of a team. Group games and sports teach children that not all people have equal skill levels and that one can have fun even if he isn't the biggest, fastest, or best at a sport.

Safety   The alone child can develop certain skills related to these games. A child can practice pitching into a net, chase a Frisbee all over the yard, jump rope, shoot baskets, and play marbles or jacks without a playmate.

Make certain that your children know how to use all sporting equipment safely and that they understand the "limits" of the court or playing field. Never allow them to play in the street; give them instructions about what to do if a ball sails over a fence, goes into the street, or lands in the neighbor's prized flower bed. Check out a vacant lot or playing field for gopher holes, broken bottles, and other potential hazards.

4 ▲ Cooking

Cooking is the one skill children can use all their lives. No matter what they choose as occupations, they'll always need to eat.

Basic Skills   Cooking can be a parent-child activity. Even young children can measure and stir. As they mature and hand-eye coordination develops, ask them to make a salad, mix a batch of cookies, or bake a cake. Your children will take pride in a task that is accomplished successfully and will enjoy both eating the finished product and receiving the praise of family members.

Teach your children to read a recipe.

Teach them basic cooking techniques—such as how to crack open an egg, turn pancakes, and measure staples.

Teach your children how to use basic kitchen appliances and utensils, including knives. It's amazing how much they can prepare in a microwave, given a little instruction.

Let your children help you with various kitchen activities, such as sorting through the beans before soaking them.

Staying Safe   Teach your kids what to do if a fire erupts (in other words, how to use the fire extinguisher that should be located in your kitchen pantry) . . . what to do if they burn or cut themselves . . . and how to safely use an oven and a stove.

Etiquette and Economics   Show your children how to set a table properly and let that be a regular chore.

Ask your kids to help with grocery shopping. You may want to give them (ten years and older) a list of three items to find in the store while you put other things into your basket. Show them how to comparison shop, read labels, and look for bargains. Make grocery shopping a challenge and your kids will hardly notice that it's also an educational experience.

Cleanup   Finally, teach them how to clean up the kitchen and let them help you after meals.

Adventures with Foods   Your children may develop a specialty as junior chefs. One young man considers himself the best spaghetti and chili man on his block. A teenage girl has developed her own version of the best chocolate cake in the world. Your teenager may want to experiment with different types of pizzas and other put-together-with-lots-of-variety meals, such as stuffed baked potatoes, nachos, and omelettes.

Children from early ages can make sandwiches and can help with preparing school lunches.

Introduce older children to new foods, new spices and herbs, and new taste combinations. They will enjoy eating a balanced diet more if they have a part in creating it and can enhance it with spices and condiments of their choosing.

Rather than allow your kids to eat junk food in front of the tube, encourage them to create nutritious food.

5 ▲ Puzzles

Children can spend hours . . . and hours . . . and hours . . . working and reworking puzzles.

Puzzles for Tots   For the little ones, select wooden puzzles with knobs. Puzzles are made of lots of materials these days, from wood to plastic to foam to furry fabric. Your children can explore the different textures.

Jigsaw Puzzles   Older children look forward to working more complicated puzzles, all the way up to extremely difficult jigsaw puzzles. They can work these by themselves or with friends.

Kids can make jigsaw puzzles, too. Pages from old magazines can be mounted on construction paper and then cut up.

Educational puzzles create the alphabet or the United States or the countries of the world.

You may want to consider a puzzle exchange with friends who have children near the ages of yours. Your children will get to try new puzzles for a few weeks, and their old puzzles will seem like familiar friends that need to be reworked once they return home.

Teach your kids to keep all the pieces to a puzzle together and to work only one puzzle at a time. (Since puzzle boxes sometimes tear easily and spill readily, keep puzzle pieces in a plastic bag.)

Three-Dimensional Puzzles

Rubik's Cubes and small metal puzzles can keep children occupied for hours at a time. They're good take-along toys as the kids accompany you on errands.

Word Puzzles

Puzzle books for children come in specialized themes or feature a specialized type of puzzle, such as jumbled-letter, crossword, and secret code puzzles. And with them, your kids will learn new vocabulary words, develop perception skills, learn to follow rules and puzzle protocols, and gain practice in spelling.

Art Puzzles

These puzzle types include mazes, connect-the-dots, and hidden pictures.

Riddles

Invest in a simple-to-read riddle book and let your children make up their own games as they quiz each other.

6 ▲ Animal Care and Training

Watching and playing with their pet will benefit kids more than watching Lassie on TV. Furthermore, the care and training of a pet can be a time-consuming activity that leaves little time for wondering what's on the tube.

Type of Pet In addition to cats and dogs, you may want to consider these pets:

- *Fish.* Children can be taught and then be required to take on the responsibility of feeding the fish, cleaning the fish bowl, and maintaining proper water chemistry.
- *Birds.* Cockatiels and parakeets can be trained in amazing ways. Again, it should become the children's responsibility to clean the cage and supply fresh water and food.
- *An ant farm.* Although these sealed, self-contained units require no maintenance, children can learn from watching the ants at work.

Guidelines Choose a pet suitable to the ages and levels of maturity of your kids, their temperaments, the area in which you live, and your willingness as an adult to help shoulder the responsibility for this particular pet.

Keep in mind that kittens become cats, puppies become dogs, bunnies become rabbits, and cute little yellow ducks become big white birds! Ducks, chickens, rabbits, and large animals are probably best left to farms and homes with sufficient acreage.

Whenever appropriate, let your kids have a say in choosing the pet. They will feel more responsibility for a pet they help to pick out.

Responsible Ownership Give children the primary responsibility for the care and training of the animal. A pet will develop children's patience and compassion. A pet will teach them limits of behavior. Furthermore, in the ongoing care of and interaction with a pet, your kids will learn about the need for proper medical care and preventive health care, about the attributes of loyalty (and that loyalty is a two-way street), about procreation and birth, and about the need for practice and more practice in developing habits and physical skills.

Pet Visitation You may choose a pet that your children visit. The pet may be a horse boarded at a farm a few miles from town, a special animal in the petting zoo, which you have affectionately named and consider to be "part of your family" even though the animal lives elsewhere, or an animal that belongs to a relative. Regular visits are a fun alternative to TV!

Consider taking your kids to a pet show, especially a show featuring their type of pet, such as a dog show, cat show, and so forth. They will get to choose their own favorites.

7 ▲ Scrapbooks

By working on a scrapbook—choosing items, organizing them, gluing them in, and so forth—children develop a sense of design, priorities, and likes and dislikes. Making a scrapbook requires creative choice and involvement with the subject matter, neither of which are required in depth by television.

Personal Interests   Is one child a sports enthusiast? She might keep a scrapbook of photos and newspaper articles about her accomplishments or those of favorite sports figures.

A young child can create a scrapbook on a particular topic. Give him old magazines so that he can cut out pictures of airplanes, cars, flowers, horses, puppies, or any pictures he likes. After all, it's his scrapbook.

For "my house" scrapbook, your child can create rooms and choose different styles and items that she'd like to see in her dream home.

Christmas Wishes   Do you receive a lot of mail-order catalogs at your house? Let your children cut them up to create their own "biggest and best just-for-me catalog" filled with all of their favorite things. Pursue this activity as Christmas looms on the horizon. However, be sure to remind the children that just as you don't buy everything you see in catalogs, so you aren't going to buy them everything you find in their catalogs.

Special Events   One child may want to make a scrapbook devoted exclusively to a vacation or to a series of vacations. Another child may devote a scrapbook specifically to birthday or holiday celebrations. Or he may want to make a scrapbook about the family—with a section for each family member.

Contents   A scrapbook could contain any of these items:

- *Favorite photographs* with time, place, and people or objects labeled
- *Ticket stubs and programs* of events your child has attended as well as ones in which she has had a part
- *Newspaper clippings* related to your child or to events, friends, or community happenings that your child considers important or memorable
- *Items that mark special events,* such as the first baby tooth that your child loses, a name tag from a special event, a first airline ticket, a photocopy of your child's first paycheck, a

dried flower from the corsage your child is given before a special dance or party

- *Original creations,* such as poems or small pieces of artwork
- *Postcards* of places visited or places your child dreams of visiting someday
- *Ribbons, medals, and certificates*—"prizes" your child receives, certificates of membership, baptism, confirmation, and so forth
- *Special letters,* perhaps from noted public figures, beloved relatives, or a respected minister or priest

8 ▲ Music Practice

It's daily.

It's noisy—and sometimes discordant.

And sometimes, it seems like forever before one senses a degree of progress.

But music practice does more than give a child a level of skill in reading music and playing an instrument.

Lessons Music practice

- develops discipline of the daily variety. Insist that your child agree to practice if you are going to pay for lessons, and that your child practice without complaint. Not everything in life is fun all the time, and not everything in life can be accomplished in a day. Both are valuable lessons.
- should be scheduled, generally on a daily basis. The scheduling of practice time teaches time management.
- encourages a child to set goals and to break them down into subgoals to accomplish them. For example, the child's goal may be to learn to play the entire score of "The En-

tertainer." A subgoal may be a certain scale or "run" or segment of the piece.

- is self-rewarding and self-reinforcing. A child generally knows when he plays the wrong note, squeaks or squawks, or misses a fingering. Repetition of a task until it is performed successfully builds patience, persistence, and a sense of personal accomplishment.
- enhances eye-hand coordination (and in some cases, eye-hand-and-foot coordination).
- helps your child discover more about potential, inherent traits and abilities, and the correlation between practice and performance.

Learning to play a string, wind, or percussion instrument prepares your child for interacting with others in a band, an orchestra, or a musical ensemble.

Vocal training is a suitable activity for children. Participation in a children's choir is a great learning experience.

Method　A new method called The Miracle teaches a child to play a keyboard linked to a computer: it provides personalized reinforced instruction. Music practice and lessons have never been so fun or so easy!

Teachers   The value of a music teacher cannot be overlooked or replaced, however. A music teacher can develop special talents or help a child overcome bad habits. A teacher can also work with a child to develop a musical ear, an appreciation for music of all types, and a knowledge of music history and theory.

Performances   Music lessons and practice seem to lead inevitably to music performance —the annual or semiannual recital. Through these performance opportunities, your child overcomes stage fright and develops skills necessary for appearing in front of an audience—skills that are readily transferred to giving a public presentation as an adult one day.

9 ▲ Watching

Kids should be observers of more than the animated box in the living room.

Bird Watching   Children of all ages can use a pair of binoculars to watch neighborhood birds, especially when nests are being built, eggs are hatching, and young birds are learning to fly. Help your kids identify birds of different types; develop their interest in the variety and unusual aspects of the natural world.

You may want to buy a book about bird species to teach the names of birds. Your children will quickly discover the differences in coloration and habits of the males and females of a species. You may also want to buy a bird-calling whistle for each child or a tape of different bird sounds. Log the names, times, and places of the birds your children spot.

You may want to put up a bird feeder, a birdbath, and a birdhouse for your backyard, patio, or balcony. Then the whole family can watch wild birds avail themselves of a meal and bath. Make your children aware of the migration of birds. They can make a car game out of spotting flocks of birds as they fly north in the spring and south in the fall.

Weather Watching   Teach your children to read the weather signs in nature; they are just as interesting as the weather reports on television. Children can learn the names of clouds and the types of formations that frequently lead to snow, rain, or violent weather. Give each child a stint at being the personal family weather reporter.

Teach them to read a thermometer and a barometer, and place versions outside. Invest in a rain gauge and teach your kids to measure precipitation. They may want to keep a log of weather-watching activities—perhaps charting temperature, cloud conditions, and whether a day is sunny or cloudy.

Your kids may observe natural weather predictors apart from the phenomena in the skies—such as the growth of bark on trees, the distinctive chirping of insects, the behavior of animals before storms, and the growth of an outdoor animal's fur coat. Give your children the current *Farmer's Almanac* and see what interesting tidbits they glean.

Star Watching   Your children can spend prime-time hours exploring the real stars instead of viewing the stars on prime-time television. You can get them started with an inexpensive telescope and a chart of the stars. You may want to include a moon calendar that shows the moon in its different phases every day of the year.

Learning about the stars gives your kids an appreciation for the vastness of the universe and the precision of the seasons as they come and go. They may want to keep a chart of daily sunrise and sunset times and notes about "falling stars," orbiting satellites, and other night-sky phenomena.

"Other" Watching   Just about anything can be watched. Position your young child's playpen in front of a sliding glass door with the drapes drawn so he can watch all of the doings of the yard or neighborhood. Animals can be watched as well as birds; look for squirrels in the trees or deer that come near the backyard for food in the winter. As you travel with your children, make "people watching" a part of your family activity. Of course, this doesn't mean staring.

10 ▲ Golf

Golf is a game for children from three to ninety-three. It's a game that both men and women can play, and they can play together. It's a game that can be played alone or in groups. It's a game that is gaining popularity worldwide. It was once a game of the socially elite, but it's now a game that has become a social equalizer.

Courses   Your kids need not play at a local course, although teenagers will probably find that to be "the" place to play. Young children can make up a golf game with just about any stick or bat and virtually any type of ball. Nerf golf and child-sized golf sets can be used for both indoor and outdoor play.

Your kids may also design their own golf course with obstacles. It can be indoors or outdoors. And some holes may overlap or crisscross others in the house or yard.

You may want to encourage your children to limit themselves to a putter and to become masters at miniature golf. A course can be con-

structed just about anywhere by moving a portable "hole" from place to place, designating a tee-
off point, and putting obstacles in between (from
pieces of furniture indoors to rocks and logs in
the backyard).

Skills   Kids can spend literally dozens of
hours a month practicing on a putting green or a
driving range. They will learn many lessons associated with other types of regular practice—
mental concentration, physical coordination, and
the relationship between practice and performance.

Alternative Games   The general game
concept of golf can be adapted to other equipment. For example, the kids may set up a Frisbee
golf course with a shallow pan or bucket as the
"hole" to hit from various tee-off points. A small
golf-style course may be set up with marbles.
They may play a large-scale version of soccer
golf; use a soccer ball instead of a golf ball and a
basket turned on its side as a hole.

Evening Play   Older children and teens
will enjoy an evening out of the house with
Mom and Dad or their friends at the night
course. Numerous courses are now lighted
for nighttime golf; some versions are played with
glowing balls.

How much better it is to breathe the air, tackle the challenge, and get the physical exercise of a real course than to sit curled up on the sofa watching the game being played on TV!

11 ▲ Concerts, Plays, and Other Live Events

Let your kids experience the thrill of live performances.

Concerts or Recitals Numerous community concerts are free, especially those for children. Many symphony orchestras have one concert a year to which the public is invited free of charge—perhaps a concert in the park or at a skating rink. Check the schedules at a nearby college or the local high school for performances by the school's band, orchestra, or choral groups. Your young musicians will not be dismayed that the quality of the performance may not be up to your trained-ear adult standards. They'll be fascinated that young people are performing the music.

Is a favorite performer coming to town? You may want to splurge for tickets. Be wary of rock concerts, however. They certainly aren't for young children. (In fact, I don't recommend them at all for children or young teenagers.)

If your children are learning to play instruments or show a special interest in one type of music, you may want to expose them to a concert featuring their instrument or favorite music. Colleges frequently hold recitals by seniors or graduate students. Small ensemble groups also perform regularly.

Many communities sponsor a children's series of concerts. Performers explain the music and display the capabilities of various instruments in an educational way for the young audience members. Children also learn about the etiquette of concert going.

Also encourage children to attend the recitals of friends. Let them learn to applaud as well as to perform. Attending a recital is one way of expressing friendship and providing moral support.

Churches frequently present musical programs —usually choir oriented—especially on Sunday evenings. Often the programs have a theme, such as patriotism, or are related to a holiday, such as Christmas.

Dramatic Performances

Churches, schools, and community theaters regularly present plays, musicals, pageants, and variety shows, many of which are suitable for family viewing. (If you have a question about the content of a show, call in advance.) In addition, some communities have a children's theater season.

Mimes sometimes frequent city parks or zoos.

Puppet shows always appeal to children.

Other Events   Although you may not think of them in the same category as a Broadway musical, circus acts offer drama and a high degree of showmanship. Take your kids to the circus.

Watch for traveling shows with characters your kids may recognize—such as the annual Sesame Street characters in concert or a Disney review performance.

Children are delighted at the antics of the Harlem Globetrotters—more show than athletic event. And an Ice Capades performance showcases skills on ice.

Children of all ages never tire of certain ballet programs, especially "The Nutcracker." Don't be surprised if you find your kids trying some of the moves they see the dancers make.

Many children are fascinated by a live performance of opera vignettes. They often sit spellbound at the power and potential of the human voice.

A live performance shows your children that mistakes and flubs are parts of real life. The perfection of television isn't the norm. This realization frees many children to take risks and to try their hands at new activities related to music and drama.

12 ▲ The Park

Discover the activities at a local park.

Lots to See and Do   Depending on its location and features, the park is a good place to investigate

- displays of artwork and craft items.
- ducks, geese, and swans swimming on the lake or pond. Take a bag of bread crumbs with you. (If your park doesn't have a pond, it may well have pigeons. They also enjoy eating what you bring.)
- merry-go-rounds, slides, large sandboxes, swings, and other playground equipment to which your children don't have access at home.
- plenty of wide-open space for running, skipping, flying a kite, or throwing a Frisbee.
- a zoo. Many parks have small zoos associated with them. In other cases, the park you visit may be primarily a zoo.
- a small ice-skating rink or perhaps a roller-skating/skateboarding cement surface or perhaps small amusement-park-style rides.

- people. Enjoy watching the grandmother pushing a pram, the grandfather dozing on a bench, the jogger huffing and puffing his way down the walk, the local group of guys playing softball, the young mothers with their children at the sandbox, the ice cream vendor with his pushcart, the skateboarders doing their tricks, the dancers practicing their moves, the child learning to roller-skate, the college kids studying while sun-bathing, and the list goes on.

Live Action   The park is a good place for your kids to run and get rid of the pent-up energy of the day, and

- to greet friends who seem to frequent the park about the same time you do each day.
- to note the changing of the seasons.
- to watch birds and squirrels.
- to fly kites.
- to yell and scream as much as they want.
- to collect pebbles and leaves and twigs.
- to play group games and sports.

The park is a good place to go when home or the yard or the balcony or the patio is too small a place to play.

13 ▲ Sewing Projects

Because sewing involves a number of steps, your kids develop a wide range of skills:

- Making choices. Choosing a pattern and fabric and matching accessory items (such as buttons or trims) is one giant exercise in decision making and creativity.
- Following a prescribed set of instructions. As children learn to read and follow a pattern, they learn about sequencing.
- Doing work precisely. Sewing is a skill that challenges kids to do high-quality work and to learn when it's best or necessary to rip it out and try again.

Along the way, eye-hand coordination is developed. Perseverance is required. And the completion of a job well done (and an item of clothing or interior decoration) becomes a point of accomplishment that enhances self-esteem.

Sewing projects help children become aware of their bodies and likes and dislikes. Over time, they develop a personal concept of style, which they may express through what they sew.

The Basics   Give your kids sewing lessons or at least teach them how to use a sewing machine. Even if they don't become masters at handwork or sewing, they need to learn to use a needle and thread and to make simple repairs or alterations to garments: to repair a ripped seam, to put in or change a hem, to replace or reinforce a button, and to patch a garment.

Other Projects   Sewing can also include these projects:

- Lacing and weaving
- Needlework, embroidery, and cross-stitch
- Knitting and crocheting
- Quilting

Several easy, quick-to-finish projects are marketed so that your children may gain more immediate gratification.

Creative Outlet   Sewing provides a wonderful creative outlet for children. They can mix and match ideas, fabrics, and garments. Even children who don't enjoy sewing clothes may enjoy sewing doll clothes and accessories or stitching a new set of curtains or pillows for the bedroom. Boys often tackle unusual sewing projects, such as adding decals and emblems to a vest or jacket or recovering a bicycle seat.

Hours spent sewing are hours spent in a creative, productive, and fun learning process—something television can't offer.

14 ▲ Radio

Radio and television may seem like brothers, but in fact, they are more like distant media cousins.

Radio engages the imagination in a way that television cannot. Just ask a person who grew up listening to radio dramas. To be sure, the Shadow *does* know, and each person has a version of what falls out of Fibber McGee's closet!

Several stations periodically play radio dramas, and cassette-tape series of some of those old shows are available in many public libraries. If they aren't in yours, you may be able to convince your librarian to order them for you or to request them through interlibrary loan.

There's more to radio, of course, than music, news, and drive-time talk shows.

A Police Scanner   Children may listen to live action as it happens "out there somewhere" in the nighttime hours.

A Multiband Radio   Explore the programming of other countries. Encourage teenagers to analyze how European radio stations interpret and prioritize news events, comparing their coverage to the way the stories are told or covered by the local network affiliate.

A Ham Radio Set   Children enjoy talking to other children in faraway places just as much as adults enjoy talking to other adults in other states and foreign lands. Preparing for licensure as a ham radio operator can be a time-consuming, skill-developing, and highly rewarding task for older children or teens. The world truly is becoming a global village, one in which English is being spoken by an increasing percentage of the villagers. Teens can have enriching experiences as they exchange ideas and information with teens in other parts of the world.

Science Kits   In addition to listening to the radio, many children accept the challenge of making radio sets. With various science kits, a child may build a radio receiver.

Walkie-Talkies   Walkie-talkies are a variation on the radio theme. You may want to encourage your children to learn Morse code and to practice sending and receiving coded messages over small radio units connecting bedrooms within your home or connecting the bedrooms of other children in your neighborhood.

15 ▲ Bubbles, Kites, and Paper Planes

Bubbles, kites, and planes can be a part of make-believe play. Kids can explore the possibilities of story lines that include flying.

Bubbles   Send your children outside with a jar of bubble juice and a few large and small wands (including a plastic ring-style holder that connects a six-pack of aluminum cans), and watch them make and blow bubbles.

Various bubble-making devices on the market include a toy camera that blows bubbles through its "lens" and other equipment that creates strings of small bubbles. Some of the larger and more elaborate wands are packaged with booklets that tell how to make oversized and unusually shaped bubbles.

(Note: Small children should be closely supervised when blowing bubbles. Bubble juice isn't for drinking!)

Kites   Right along with bubbles in the arena of wind-play toys are kites. Visit your local toy store and you'll quickly conclude that kites aren't what they used to be. There are multiple kites and kites for trick flying. Some require quite a bit of skill; teenagers will be challenged!

Kites generally require some assembly. Kite making provides yet another exercise for kids in learning to follow instructions.

Make certain that your kids know kite-flying safety rules and that they have plenty of open space in which to fly a kite—far away from electrical wires, television antennas, and trees.

Paper Planes   Encourage your kids to try their hands at making paper planes. With certain kits, children can make fairly large planes. They can learn engineering at a very practical level as they build a plane and experiment with flying it.

Although they are expensive and definitely not for young children, motorized planes that are maneuvered either by guide wires or by remote control devices can teach various skills. Again, an open space is required away from crowds.

16 ▲ Museums and Galleries

Most museums and galleries across the country have learned that tomorrow's patrons of the arts are today's children. Many offer exhibits specifically for children.

Museums   Your kids will be fascinated by a visit to a museum that features

- dinosaur bones and other prehistoric exhibits.
- exhibits of props and costumes from well-known children's movies.
- exhibits with working parts. A number of science and technology museums have special areas in which children can conduct on-site experiments.

Some museums are designed for children. Exhibits are presented simply with explanations that children understand, and there are lots of hands-on activities. Look for them as you travel on vacation. Or if you live in a large city, periodically visit them.

Galleries   Although young children may get bored in an art gallery, older children will enjoy the occasional visit, especially if you see a limited number of paintings that you've researched and discussed in advance. The paintings and pieces of sculpture will have more meaning for children if you've talked with them about the life and times of the painter or sculptor.

Every child is an artist. As a kindergartner, a child excels in painting. As you explore fine paintings, talk them over with your children. Get up close and look at how the colors are put together. Ask questions about the paintings; ask your kids to choose favorites and then tell you why they made those choices.

Other Exhibits   In many ways, a zoo or an aquarium can be considered a gallery. And what child doesn't love a visit to see the animals and fish. Go often. Your children will discover something new each time.

Take advantage of special exhibits that come to your city, for example, a car show or a boat show.

Words of Advice   Keep in mind as you explore museums and galleries that your children will always be most interested in (1) things that move, (2) things they can manipulate, (3) things to which they can relate (that is, things that are part of their everyday world), and (4) exhibits related to a story line. Even so, their attention span is limited. Don't try to do an entire gallery, museum, or show in a day. Give yourself an hour or two at the most. Leave while your children are still full of curiosity. They will be more eager to return to the gallery or museum the next time you suggest an outing there.

17 ▲ Typing Practice

Typing is a prerequisite to success in various fields, especially in the world of computers (including word processing, marketing, economic forecasting, scientific formulations, and statistical monitoring).

Furthermore, your budding high-school and college students will find good typing skills to be a lifesaver when they have to prepare term papers. Some students might even turn those skills into a part-time job or a way to help friends.

Learn the Right Way   Children are exposed to keyboards at an early age. That makes it even more important for them to learn to type accurately with good form that can lead to fast speeds.

Get a typing instruction booklet, and encourage your kids to practice. Daily. Without looking at the keyboard. It may take twenty minutes a day for six months before they become adept at typing. In the years ahead, your kids will thank you many times over for insisting that they acquire this skill.

What if You Don't Have a Typewriter?

Scour the flea markets. Look through newspaper ads. Talk to people in repair outlets that specialize in computers or typewriters. In other words, look for a bargain. Outdated computer systems and typewriters (manual, electric, and electronic) are frequently available for just a fraction of their original price. The keyboard unit you purchase may not be one you'd want to use for projects that need a highly professional look, but it can be great for learning to type.

Typing can be learned in the time it takes to watch one TV sitcom for one thirteen-week series of programs, most of which your children will not be able to recall by this time next year. Redeem the time.

18 ▲ Collection Building

Most children seem to be pack rats. Frequently, the "precious things" take on a certain similarity or tend to focus on a particular interest. Voilà! A child has a collection!

What's in It?   A child can build a collection of virtually anything:

- Stamps
- Butterflies (or other insects)
- Rocks (highly polished or as found, cut or whole, gemstone or garden variety)
- Shells (exotic or beach fare)
- Coins (although this is frequently too expensive for a child's collecting, apart from pennies)
- Dolls
- Teddy bears (or stuffed animals in general)
- Old keys
- Stickers
- Postcards

Some children collect a certain type of figurine, such as clowns or horses.

Certainly, a valuable and useful collection is that of books, especially sets of favorite children's books.

Collections can be of the nature walk variety—feathers, leaves, or seed pods.

Many children collect cards, such as baseball cards or the relatively new cards of the astronauts.

Girls often collect charms for a bracelet or necklace. Boys frequently collect caps or T-shirts.

Christmas ornaments can be collected and displayed each year. Ultimately, the set can go with the grown child as he or she establishes a home.

Helpful Hints   Emphasize the joy of the hunt more than the acquisition. Let your children have a good time searching for items on their own.

Focus on items that are fairly inexpensive. Ideally, children should use their own money, with some items coming as gifts from parents or other relatives.

Help kids identify an item that they truly enjoy using, looking at, or reading about. Try to find an item that will hold their interest for several years.

Building a collection gives kids a sense of accomplishment, of perseverance (finding that one last rare item), and it promotes a desire to conduct research into a particular area. In addition, your kids can sometimes learn about the financial aspects of collecting and dealing in collectibles.

You can spur on the collecting interest by finding books about the items they are collecting.

Children should organize and display their collections. For example, they may put postcards, stickers, or baseball cards in albums. In some cases, they may have to be inventive.

19 ▲ Library Exploration

Your local community library has far more than books. Encourage your kids to explore the library fully. Take them there for an occasional outing.

Tapes   Ask about collections of audiotapes or videotapes. Sometimes you can find rare tapes of early television programs, special concerts, documentaries of special events in history, or science programs. Many times, these are unavailable in the video stores. The best news is that they can nearly always be checked out free or at a reduced fee. Sometimes viewing or listening rooms are available.

Music   Ask about the music section. Your children have little familiarity with records—those of the 33 rpm and 45 rpm variety that you once thought were the newest and latest in recording innovation. Explore the old-time greats with your kids. Share the oldie-but-goody music you liked as well as the records your kids' grandparents and perhaps even great-grandparents enjoyed. Broaden your kids' musical horizons.

Visual Aids   Ask about slides and other collections of visual material. Research an upcoming vacation or help your kids with projects about far-away places.

Computers   Many libraries have computers with a wide range of educational software packages for public use.

Periodicals   Browse through the periodicals section. You'll find many more titles there than at any newsstand. Look for magazines that specialize in an area of interest to your kids. Children's magazines are frequently available.

Nonfiction   Consider going to the library with a specific list of questions or topics for you and your children to look up together in the nonfiction section. Wander the stacks together in search of "the answer." Don't wait for a homework assignment. Be enthused about learning for learning's sake.

Behavior   Teach your kids library etiquette, such as how to move about quietly and to speak softly when making requests or asking questions. Show them where the restrooms and drinking fountain are located so they can use them on their own. Teach them how to request information from a librarian, how to use a card catalog (or other filing system), where to browse for certain types of books, and how to be a friend both to the librarian and to other patrons using the library.

Spending an occasional evening at your local library can be a relaxing, yet enlightening time for parents and kids alike. There's one thing a library has that television doesn't: quiet. It's an atmosphere your kids will benefit from experiencing.

20 ▲ Research Projects

Closely related to library visits are research projects. These can take on several forms for children. Always begin with their interests or questions. Stimulate their curiosity and then help them find answers on their own.

Resources   Most questions or topics won't require kids to delve into all these resources. At other times, they may want to read entire books on a subject or take a course of sorts in a field.

Use Reference Books   Find out what is said in books and encyclopedias. Consult a dictionary frequently. Teach your children to look up words they don't understand or know how to spell.

Use Maps   When a nation is mentioned on the news or at a church missions conference or in a conversation, find it on the map. Discuss the importance of its location and note its proximity to other nations. Use a variety of maps to explore the culture, topography, and natural resources of the area.

Use Magazines Become familiar with the *Readers' Guide to Periodical Literature* as a means of finding current information. Especially look for articles that have pictures or illustrations to further pique the curiosity of your kids. If the language of the article is beyond their reading level, paraphrase the information.

Identify Experiments With science kits from archaeology to zoology, your kids can conduct experiments on their own or with friends. Be cautious, however, when it comes to chemistry sets, and always keep such kits out of the reach of young children.

Talk to Experts and Go on Field Trips Together If a child shows a special interest in a particular profession or topic, you may want to seek out a person in that profession and ask for a brief interview. Go with questions prepared in advance and written down for your reference during the interview. Ask about how the person does the job, what training was required to prepare for the job, and what he sees as the benefits of his work (both to himself and to society).

Search Out Special Public Exhibits, Museums, or Other Places of Interest Don't overlook planetariums, botanical gardens, zoos, aquariums, historical museums, galleries, and special technology shows as places where your kids can find examples to look at and experts to talk to.

Travel   As you travel, stop by national monuments and parks and enjoy the programs available for public viewing. Your children can learn from these free exhibits and media programs.

Diversions   Research projects, of course, don't need to focus on academic subjects. Your kids may be most interested in pursuing sports trivia or looking up the answer to a question about a hobby. For that matter, a shopping trip can provide an exercise in comparison research as you and your kids look for the best buy (weighing such factors as price, quality, durability, serviceability, and so forth).

Family   Tell children about a family tree. They can discover their ancestors as well as learn more about the nation and continent where ancestors once lived.

21 ▲ Parlor Games

Turn off the TV game shows and get out the game boards.

What They Can Play Teach your kids to play the familiar favorites, and occasionally play these games with them:

- Checkers and Chinese checkers
- Chess
- Monopoly (consider, too, the fairly new version of Monopoly for children)
- Card games (such as Rook, Old Maid, Fish, Authors, or 21)
- Scrabble or Scrabble Junior or other word games
- Trivial Pursuit (also with children's versions)
- Pictionary
- Other board games (such as Candyland, Uncle Wiggly, Chutes and Ladders, and Sorry!)

New games are being invented all the time. Periodically explore your local game store or toy shop.

When They Can Play   As you travel, consider taking along magnetic or pegged versions of checkers and chess.

Children can fill up spare minutes such as those in waiting rooms by playing a quiet game of Hangman or Tick-tack-toe.

What They Learn   Parlor games teach children that competition isn't always limited to physical skills or brute force. They also learn how to take turns, how to lose gracefully, how to work with a partner (in certain games) and, in some cases, how to reason mathematically or develop strategy skills.

22 ▲ Hide-and-Seek

By playing hide-and-seek, kids develop perception skills as well as gain a sense of control over play action (especially when they hide themselves or an object).

If you are playing along, or if your time for play is limited, make sure your children understand that they must respond to your call or designated signal. This is especially important if you are playing outdoors or in an unfamiliar location. Also make certain that at least one person stays put as a home base at all times. All participants should be able to find their way "home."

Just as much fun as playing the "human" version of hide-and-seek can be playing I Spy. A designated object in a room is selected as the goal of the game, and each person asks questions that lead to its identity.

Away from Home As a travel game or a game to take along on a visit to a doctor's office or dental clinic, make a list of items in advance for your kids to look for during the excursion. (The list can be long or short, depending on the length of your trip. You may want to make a new list for each day of a multiday journey.) As a child spots items, mark those items off the list, or put the child's initials next to them. The goal of the game may be to find all of the items or to see which child finds the most items. The game takes your kids' minds off the length of a trip or distracts them from fear or concern associated with a trip to the doctor or dentist.

In the Neighborhood   Another variation on the hide-and-seek theme is to send your kids out into the yard or neighborhood to find a list of items or note the location of various items. For example, ask them to make a note of something yellow, to describe where you can find the rose-bush with the most roses in bloom on it, to count the number of blue cars parked in your apartment complex parking lot, or to count the number of bird's nests in the trees on your block.

In Their Rooms   Yet another variation on the hide-and-seek game is to send your kids into their rooms to find certain objects. This is an especially effective way to preface a demand that they clean up their rooms.

23 ▲ Creative Performances

Challenge your children and their friends to prepare a performance.

Play Suggest one based on a holiday theme, such as Thanksgiving or the Fourth of July. Let your children

- write the play.
- design the costumes.
- create the props and sets.
- make up the programs.
- do fliers for distribution to family members and friends.
- design lighting and special effects (including selection of musical interludes).
- choreograph or block moves.
- conduct rehearsals.

This activity may take several days.

Variety Show Encourage each child to work up an act.

Concert   Your children may want to create a show based on their favorite songs and come up with their own choreography and lip-syncing performances of them.

Puppet Show   Socks decorated with yarn and buttons will do for puppets. Again, children make up their scripts and develop their characterizations, sets, and special effects.

TV Show   Given the technology of the age, the performance your kids and their friends create may very well be a videotape. Older children are adept at using camcorders, especially with adult supervision. Encourage them to develop a video script and then shoot it in sequence (to avoid editing) after carefully designing each segment and rehearsing it fully.

Parade   Although not always considered a performance, a parade qualifies as an event that requires planning and showmanship and prompts audience applause. Suggest that your kids and their friends create a neighborhood parade to include all the children.

Neighborhood Fair   Children can put together booths and invite the neighbors to admire their handiwork and artwork, view their collections, buy their cookies and cakes, and play their games (from darts to fishing with magnets for small prizes). Pets—in cages, of course—can be admired and judged in a pet show competition. Prompt your kids to come up with a way to make every entry a winner.

Competitions   Children can plan and sponsor a neighborhood, church group, or club tournament—a chess tournament or a swim meet, their own version of the Olympics (with such team sports as handball, and such individual sports as a fifty-yard dash), a marbles, jacks, or yo-yo competition, or perhaps a contest for mud castles. Again, prompt your children to find a way of applauding each competitor.

24 ▲ Nature Walks

Go for a walk. A walk provides a means of exercise and a release from the stress of the workday (including the workday spent doing housework). And a walk provides a time together for children and adults.

Talk   Notice things around you as you walk. Comment on them. Point out new or unusual things, including the blooming flowers, the branch that fell during the storm, and various signs that indicate a change of season.

You can also talk over the day. Explore what went on in your kids' lives even as you explore your neighborhood.

Visit with Neighbors   Pause to share ideas or news with those you find working in their yards. You'll probably come home with at least one new idea.

Take Note of Nature Where You Find It
Talk to the neighborhood dog. Watch the squirrels play in the trees. Observe the birds as they settle down for the evening. Pause to consider the

ants and beetles and butterflies. Call attention to the beauty of cloud formations or the glory of a sunset. Inhale deeply.

At times, you may want to draw conclusions or make comments about what you see on your walk. At other times, you may want to walk in silence and absorb the moment visually.

You'll find that your kids look forward to these times when they can count on being with you. They'll find comfort in exploring aspects of their neighborhood with you. And they'll especially enjoy a late-night walk as something unusual and exciting.

Walk in Other Areas   From time to time, take a walk through a community park. Or visit a local botanical garden or nature preserve. Try to visit such an area at least once a season. Notice the changes from visit to visit. Build into your kids an awareness of the beauty associated with each season.

Drive out in the country and walk along country roads, forest trails, or lakes and rivers. You'll return home feeling as if you've been on a mini-vacation, and chances are, your children won't miss the regularly scheduled programming of that night.

25 ▲ Journal Writing

Keeping a journal or a diary, making periodic entries, has several benefits for your children.

Your Children Develop Language Skills
They will become more adept at expressing themselves in writing and will probably find that writing becomes less a chore and more a delight. This is a chance for your kids to develop a style of written communication, to practice penmanship, and to feel a need for a greater vocabulary.

Your Children Record Comings and Goings, Accomplishments, and Activities As children look back over a journal, they frequently have a sense of personal growth and of trends in their lives, even though any single day may seem fairly routine or boring. They may want to keep lists of books read, movies seen, places gone, and so forth.

Your Children Express Pent-up Feelings
The journals of children are frequently punctuated by bursts of anger, frustration, "puppy love" feelings, and great affection—all of which are part of the growing-up process. Putting these

feelings in writing is a way of releasing them and channeling them outward in a positive way.

Your children may want to include personal sketches or artwork. They may want to write poetically at times.

A Journal Can Take Many Forms

1. *Diary.* Diaries are places to note feelings as well as events and activities.

2. *Dreams.* In a journal, a child can sort out recurring, disturbing, or frightening dreams.

3. *Lists.* Sometimes the lists can be of feelings, activities, names of friends and others encountered at school and play. Sometimes the lists can relate to goals and ideas and future plans.

4. *Questions.* The journal may include a section of questions that a child is pondering.

Permit your children to keep their journals personal and private. Don't snoop. If you are also keeping a journal, you may want to share a portion of it from time to time, which opens the door for your children to share theirs with you.

Emotions and ideas are best expressed. When they are retained, they can erupt into frustration, anxiety, worry, fear, doubt, or other types of distress. Journal writing allows kids something that television inhibits: the opportunity to create words and give voice to the inner self.

26 ▲ Model Making

Through model building, children

- learn to follow instructions. Models must be built in sequence.
- develop patience. Painted pieces must dry before they can be glued together; certain glued-together pieces must dry before they can be combined. The process can take many days.
- learn perseverance. When children stick with a task until it is finished, they reinforce habits of discipline. The completed projects build up self-esteem and confidence.
- develop small motor skills. Models require precision and manipulation of small pieces.

Cars and Planes   By making model cars and airplanes, children can learn about the working and design of the real things. In addition, they can learn about twentieth-century history as they make planes and cars representative of certain eras. (Models of planes and cars are yet another type of collection your children might want to build.)

Working Models Children can build working models, such as a radio set, a robot that responds to commands, and a small pump that moves water.

Some types of construction sets can be used to make models of various types of machinery, such as cranes and elevators. Children can design, create, and then manipulate items they've constructed.

Science With the Invisible Man and Invisible Woman kits, children can paint and then put together the organs of the body within a clear plastic casing. These models teach about anatomy and are useful in explaining certain medical treatments or physical ailments to children.

With models of skeletons of dinosaurs, children can create prehistoric creatures.

Joint Effort Model building is an activity that parents and children can do together—assuming, of course, that you are wise enough to let the children assign labor to you. Let them make all the decisions about paint color and the positioning of decals. One of the best things a parent can do is to watch, applaud, and engage in conversation about the item that a child is making.

Provide a place where kids can work on models until they are completed. Make sure that other children keep their hands off the projects and don't interfere with the building process. And by all means, keep small model pieces and glue away from young children.

Once models are completed, display them. You may want to build shelves just for the purpose of displaying completed models.

27 ▲ Scouting and Other Groups for Children

Television is most often a solitary, passive activity for children. Channel your children's abundant energy, instead, into something that is active and that includes other children. Few alternatives are as valuable or as personally rewarding as membership in a Scouting organization.

Organizations   *Boy Scouts* and *Girl Scouts* prepare youngsters to feel a sense of responsibility for their communities, a sense of control over their own safety (both in the city and in the wild), and a sense of community with their peers that is positive, nonexclusive, and rooted in service.

Camp Fire Boys and Girls is another fine program, with virtually the same benefits as Scouts and an emphasis on WO-HE-LO . . . work, health, and love.

Royal Rangers is a church-based organization, as are several others you may want to explore for your children.

Growth   In virtually all of these organizations children may work their way up several ranks and earn badges, beads, or emblems along the way. Children learn specific skills useful throughout life, and they gain information that is enriching and builds self-esteem. They grow mentally, emotionally, and socially.

A Helping Hand   Single parents frequently find that Scouting programs fill a niche for their children—providing a surrogate father figure for a young son or a mother figure for a young daughter. Get to know the troop leader; you'll want your children to belong to a unit in which the other parents are involved, and you'll want your children associating with children whose families share the values you consider important.

In addition to Scouting programs, you may want to learn about a Big Brother or Big Sister program. Although these organizations are purely aimed at fostering a relationship between a child and an adult—without tasks, achievements, and group activities—the programs are extremely valuable for children who need a positive friendship with an admired, older role model.

28 ▲ Practice Ranges

Practice may not result in perfection, but children certainly get a lot closer to it if they do practice.

Tennis   Do you have a budding young tennis player in your family? Take her to a court that has a backboard against which she can hit . . . and hit . . . and hit. Buy a bucket of used balls from a local tennis club and let her practice her serve until she is satisfied with her performance.

Baseball   Do you have a child interested in baseball? Save your quarters and let him spend time at a local batting range.

Golf   Is your child learning to play golf? Both practice putting greens and driving ranges are available.

Bowling   Is your child part of a bowling league? Many bowling establishments open their lanes for morning practice sessions, especially during the summer months, at reduced rates.

Firearms   Seminars sponsored by the local police and sheriff departments teach first and foremost that guns are *not* toys. They offer instruction in the safe and correct use of several types of firearms. Teens are frequently fascinated with guns, and these seminars direct that interest into a positive recreational skill, such as skeet shooting. Safe supervised firing ranges can be found in virtually every major city.

Archery   On the archery range, children can develop skills in accuracy and distance.

29 ▲ Conversation

Turn off the tube and talk to your kids. You may all be amazed at what you discover.

Don't have the television on during mealtimes. Use meals as a time for family communication. Linger over the dinner table and talk.

- Let every person share the foremost events of the day and explore related feelings and opinions.
- Discuss and evaluate events or experiences you've shared as a family.
- Plan future events and activities as a family.
- Share the news of the day. "Did you hear about . . . ?" and "Did you hear the news today that . . . ?" are opening lines for conversations that can be far-ranging in topic— from international political news to reports of new inventions and scientific discoveries to the announcement that a frequently used nearby road is being closed for resurfacing.

Spend a few minutes with each child at bedtime. Communicate on a one-to-one basis.

Beliefs and Values   Conversations are opportunities for sharing, in an ongoing, natural way, your opinions, values, and beliefs. Don't wait until a crisis hits or a problem arises to share with your children what you believe to be fair and just behavior.

Feelings   Conversations are opportunities to share with your family how you feel about events and activities. Let your children know when certain news makes you feel sad, happy, or confused. Let them see a full range of honest emotions from you and discover that talking about one's feelings is both acceptable behavior and a beneficial process.

Family Ties   Conversations are ways in which your children will discover you as a person and each other as distinctive, uniquely gifted, and valued people. Share anecdotes from your past when they are appropriate. Let your children know that you have a reason for saying, "I can relate to that." You may want to share incidents from the lives of your parents and grandparents. Through conversations, children learn about their heritage—their family tree, their community history, their church denomination roots.

Debates   Don't let your conversations dwell on topics that irritate or cause anger in one or more family members. A vigorous heated debate about politics should end with a friendly handshake. Debate is good for children to hear; encourage their participation. Make certain the debate is based on facts, however, and not just hunches. Encourage children to have evidence to support opinions. They will emerge from such conversations with lots to think about and a better developed ability to reason.

Humor   Conversations frequently erupt in laughter. Make jokes and amusing stories and anecdotes a part of your conversations. Family members that laugh together are rich indeed.
Converse

- as you travel by car.
- as you run errands around town.
- as you sit in waiting rooms.
- as you prepare meals together.
- as you work on home-related chores with your kids.

Your children will develop both listening and speaking skills and will gain in self-respect.

30 ▲ Seasonal Sports

Activity is a key word. Television offers action but not activity. Kids need to spend growing-up years in motion. Turn your sports fans into participants.

Fishing   Take them fishing. Teach them how to bait a hook, cast a line, and reel in a fish. Teach your children safety around the water. Some cities have small man-made lakes specifically designed for teaching and practicing fishing skills.

Snow-Related Activities   In winter, if you live in an area where it snows, encourage your children to turn off the TV and to go outside for sledding . . . cross-country skiing . . . snowman building . . . or ice-skating (preferably at a supervised rink). Ice-skating, of course, can be a year-round activity. Many rinks are located in permanent structures, including shopping malls.

Water Sports   In summer, take your kids to the community swimming pool for lessons. Make certain that they learn to swim and learn safety rules around water. Summer is also a time when children go boating with adults or in their own rowboats. Again, make certain that they know the safety rules and wear life vests whenever they are in boats.

Leagues   Your children may want to join a community softball or T-ball league. The good news about T-ball is that every child gets to hit the ball and run the bases. Both boys' and girls' leagues are available just about everywhere. Call your local park service.

Soccer leagues are popular in most towns and cities. A number of large cities have basketball leagues, too.

Lessons   In addition to group sports, you may want to give your children lessons in tennis, golf, ice-skating, roller-skating, gymnastics, or another sport in which they express interest.

31 ▲ Art Projects

Art projects can keep kids busy any time of year.

Crayons and paper are musts for children. You may also want to supply a large pad of colorful construction paper, blunt-end scissors, glue, and an easel.

Consider these projects for your kids:

- Painting with water colors or tempera paints
- Working with clay, Play-Doh, or plaster kits
- Drawing with a Magnadoodle, Etch-a-Sketch, or other drawing kit
- Designing cars and other vehicles with a child's version of a T square and templates
- Making designs on paper with rubber or sponge stamps, stickers, and glitter
- Using a Colorforms kit for experimenting with designs and colors
- Designing clothes (with help from a kit)
- Making party decorations, centerpieces, or Christmas tree ornaments
- Learning the art of paper cutting or making items from papier-mâché
- Making small items of apparel or items for

home use with a small weaving kit or bead-craft kit

- Learning to knot string into macramé designs

Face Painting   Face paints are popular with children, as are kits that teach how to paint clown faces.

Sidewalk Painting   Large chunks of sidewalk chalk come in a wide variety of colors so your children can create large-scale murals on a driveway, patio, or sidewalk—all of which can be washed away easily.

Collages   Collages of photographs, of favorite things cut from old magazines, of discarded labels from cans and jars, of things brought home from nature are all possibilities. Works of art can be made from buttons, seeds, feathers, leaves, small strips of bark, and scraps of various types of wood.

Classes   Check with your local park service or community center about art classes that may be offered during summer months or on Saturdays.

Recycling   Kids can turn everyday discarded objects into useful items. For example, what could they do with glass jars? You may want to cut large detergent or cereal boxes to create hold-ers for magazines or special school papers. Let children decorate them with paper, seals, and other "glitz." What could children create from egg cartons, milk cartons, or small pieces of fab-ric or wood?

Making a Place

Prepare an area of your home or yard where children can be as messy as they need to be as they create their works of art. Set aside a T-shirt that's just for painting, or make or buy an artist's smock to protect clothing. Teach children how to pick up after a project is completed.

Also designate a place for displaying their latest creations. It may be your refrigerator door or a bulletin board.

32 ▲ Treasure Hunts

Do your children ever come to you and moan, "We're bored"? Challenge them to create a treasure hunt. The point of the hunt, of course, is for children to move from clue to clue to find a hidden treasure.

"Treasure Isle" Let children take turns coming up with clues and hiding them for one another. Limit the "treasure isle"—perhaps designating the backyard, the living room, the apartment complex, or the block on which you live as the place in which all clues and the treasure must be hidden. Suggest that your children select the final hiding place first and then work backward to choose interim spots and create clues.

The treasure itself may be quite small (and may not even be something you'd normally think of as a treasure).

The clues may be done in rhyme or as riddles. Encourage the participants to be as clever as possible in their clues.

The hunt may involve a dozen clues and interim stops or only one or two clues and stops.

Party Fun   A treasure hunt is an excellent birthday party activity (with the treasure being the cache of birthday presents hidden someplace in the house while the children pursue clues outside). A treasure hunt is also a good rainy day activity.

You may want to surprise your children with a treasure hunt of your own creation from time to time. Put out several clues that lead to a new accessory item, cassette tape, or other small gift item. Let them enjoy the thrill of the hunt.

33 ▲ Water Games

An alternative to TV viewing may be as close as the nearest water faucet.

Bathtime Soap crayons are fairly new on the market; at bathtime, kids can turn the tile or fiberglass walls around the tub into an art canvas. Various water toys, including washable dolls, water pumps, and sponge building blocks, are fun and safe for bathtub play.

Toys Squirt guns will always be a favorite. Some newer models are creative in design— trumpeting elephants and long-necked ostriches, among others.

Water toys, such as waterway transportation systems that accommodate toy boats, are popular with children.

The Garden Hose Garden hose "battles" and sprinkler play serve double duty in the summertime. The kids get cooled off, and the lawn gets watered.

Pool Play   If your kids have access to a swimming pool, they can swim with fins, learn to use a snorkel and goggles, and play with inner tubes. A net across a pool sets up a game of water volleyball for older children and teens. Water polo is a great group activity in a swimming pool. Children enjoy playing Simon Says or Follow the Leader in the pool: if one child does a certain jump or dive, the other children must follow suit. Make certain they take swimming lessons and learn about water safety rules.

Sports   Children are enthusiastic about waterskiing, rafting, and boating. Make certain they wear life vests when in a boat and they are reminded frequently of the rules for boating safety.

Carwash   You might turn washing the family car into a water game. It won't be such a chore if kids know it's OK to get soaked and have a little fun at the same time.

34 ▲ Exercise

Even beyond the playing of sports and engaging in physical activity is exercise. Although you may think that children are always on the go, the reality is that a decreasing percentage of our nation's children qualify as being physically fit. While parents are jogging or working out at a gym, their children are frequently at home mesmerized by the family television set.

Foot Power   Whenever possible, encourage your kids to run or skip. Let them run ahead of you for a hundred yards and then run back to you. It's a great way for them to release pent-up emotions, and running-jumping-skipping children tend to sleep more soundly, too.

Invite young children to go jogging with you occasionally. Parents and teenagers can race-walk, jog, and run together.

Jump to It!   Buy your kids jump ropes. If they become restless or fidgety at the lack of activity, suggest that they go jump up and down a couple of dozen times.

Moving Indoors   What about those cooped-up days of winter? Invest in a minitrampoline for your house, and let your kids jump to their hearts' content. Suggest to your young teenager that she ride your exercise bike while she's talking with her friends on the phone.

35 ▲ Creative Writing

Making up stories is an alternative to watching the stories that others have written for television.

Writers learn by writing. As your kids write, they'll learn more about the fine art of story-telling, about how to express themselves creatively, and about the differences in literary genres.

Poetry   Challenge your young child to try his hand at writing a poem. Challenge your teen to compose her own rhythmic rhyme. Bear in mind that poetry is meant to be read. Periodically have a reading hour with your family in which each member shares something aloud, preferably a personal composition.

Songs   Challenge your child to make up the lyrics and tune of a song and to sing it. Challenge your teen to notate the song and give it harmony. (They'll be even more successful at notation and harmony, of course, if they've had music lessons.)

Scripts   Challenge your children to write a play, including ideas for characterization, settings, costumes, and lighting or special effects. It's just one short step from a play to a teleplay. Challenge them to write video scripts for favorite TV characters.

Give them an opportunity to perform the play with friends or other members of your family.

Challenge your children to write a script that ties together—in a creative and fast-paced way—the slides you took on your last vacation.

Word Plays   Challenge your kids to write riddles or haiku word pictures or a series of Hebrew-style proverbs. (If you don't know what haiku is, or the rudiments of Hebrew-style proverb writing, embark on a research project.)

Computer Literacy   If your children have access to a computer, they can practice writing on it. Typing skills will be enhanced along the way. In fact, you might insist that they spend as much time writing on the computer as they do playing games.

Much of "school writing" is limited to essays. Writing at home is a different type of activity that gives wings to creativity.

36 ▲ Memory Work

Memorizing can be an activity with rich dividends. Your children will be far more adept at learning lines for a school play or pageant and will become more comfortable speaking aloud in front of others. Self-confidence and self-esteem will grow as they see that they can commit something you consider important to memory.

The passages children memorize enrich their thought life. The passages can give rise to new ideas, provide comfort in times of crisis or sorrow, and be a part of thought processes as they weigh a decision.

What to Consider   Challenge your children to memorize some of the following:

- Tongue twisters
- Poems (Learning " 'Twas the Night Before Christmas" is the ultimate challenge for many young people!)
- Famous cultural or historical documents (such as the preamble to the Constitution or the Gettysburg Address or the "We Believe" statement of your church)

- Speeches from famous plays—for example, Hamlet's "to be or not to be" monologue
- Scripture passages—such as the Twenty-Third Psalm, the Ten Commandments, or the beatitudes
- Proverbs and wise sayings
- Prayers that are the cornerstone of your faith (such as the Shema or the Lord's Prayer)

Challenge your children to learn all the verses to "Jingle Bells," your favorite Christmas carol, or a favorite hymn. Teach them the lyrics to songs that you enjoyed as a child or teen.

How to Do It   Teach children to break down a passage into short segments and to build one passage upon the next like building blocks.

Encourage them to repeat and repeat and repeat a phrase or passage in committing it to memory.

Give children an opportunity to rehearse what they have learned before you in a nonthreatening atmosphere.

37 ▲ Rest

Teachers frequently complain that students are too tired to concentrate in class. One of the foremost reasons is that they've stayed up too late watching television.

Get Sleep   Insist that sleep has priority over a TV program. With the occasional exception of a special program, set a bedtime for your kids and stick with it, no matter what's on, how many other children will be watching the show, or how exciting your kids are certain a program will be.

   Television programs frequently stimulate children and put them in a "hyper" mode mentally and emotionally, which makes sleep difficult. Turn off the television set well in advance of bedtime.

Reduce Noise   Many families are becoming increasingly noise weary. After a busy day of traffic, construction sounds, city noise, or school playground noise—with all the attendant bells and crashes and honks and clanking—home should be a place of quiet. Create a peaceful atmosphere in your home by turning off the tube.

Nap   Get children to take naps or have quiet times. Send them to bed with a book or puzzle and insist that they rest quietly for a half hour. If they don't want to read or work a puzzle, encourage them to daydream.

Daydream   Daydreaming is beneficial for children. It allows them to

- try on different roles for themselves—envisioning themselves in various places and positions and careers and, in the process, discovering what is comfortable and what is uncomfortable as they think things through.
- make up creative stories—including dialogue with imaginary friends or among imagined characters.
- project their futures—weighing choices, setting goals, and mapping out plans for reaching those goals.
- recall favorite memories.

The child who is able to daydream is a child who is rarely bored.

Pray   Encourage your kids to use rest time or before-you-go-to-sleep time to pray. It is also a good time to take a mental vacation—to concentrate on happy places and events.

Consider rest time to be good for the bodies and the souls of your children.

38 ▲ Craft Projects

By completing quality craft projects, children develop a sense of self-worth, of accomplishment, of pride in a job well done. Craft projects build the abilities to follow instructions and to put objects together in a way that is structurally sound and aesthetically pleasing. Craft projects stimulate creativity. And they give you opportunities to spend quality time with your children.

Kits Children can have fun with these kit activities:

- Building a birdhouse or a bird feeder or a birdbath
- Making and decorating a doll house, including simple pieces of furniture or accessories
- Making small wooden toys for a younger brother or sister
- Growing crystals
- Making an origami masterpiece or putting together an architectural paper model

Woodworking   Junior carpentry kits are readily available, with tools scaled down for small hands, so that boys and girls may build things with wood and learn how to use a hammer, saw, drill, screwdriver, and other household tools. One of the simplest and easiest things they can learn to build is a rectangular step stool—a practical item that requires several different woodworking skills and principles.

Other Ideas   Suggest some of these projects to your kids:

- Stringing beads together in unusual patterns to create necklaces and bracelets, using plastic or wooden beads
- Making molded figures from plaster and then painting them—for example, making a nativity set
- Lacing shapes together to create purses, key holders, and eyeglass cases
- Decorating clear plastic or wooden boxes with painted designs or glued-on shells, party glitz items, buttons, or other items of their choosing
- Stenciling fabrics and painting or stitching decorative emblems to T-shirts, sweatshirts, or tennis shoes
- Pressing flowers (and leaves) and using them to create stationery

Gifts   Craft projects can be turned into meaningful and much appreciated gifts for grandparents, aunts and uncles, or teachers. When they spend time making a craft project that they give away, kids learn the true meaning of a "gift of time" and learn to value more highly the handmade gifts they receive.

39 ▲ Bicycling

Bicycling helps children acquire balance. They get a sense of control and power as they choose where to pedal and how quickly. As your children exercise, they explore the neighborhood and spend time with other children.

Mechanical Device A bicycle is very often a child's introduction to the way mechanical devices work. Realigning a bicycle chain, inflating a bicycle tire, and adjusting a bicycle's brakes can be good opportunities for teaching the basics of vehicle maintenance and repair.

Personal Choice A bicycle is also a means of personal expression. With so many models on the market, the selection of a bicycle to a child is a little like the selection of an automobile to an adult. Go with your child as he looks at bikes, tries them out, and finally settles on a favorite. Teach him how to comparison shop for a bike and how to weigh various factors in deciding what makes a bike "good." Discuss the bicycle accessories, and allow your child to choose them or to purchase them from money he earns or saves from an allowance. He'll treat his bike with greater respect and take better care of it if he has a vested interest.

Traffic Know-How   A bicycle is your child's introduction to traffic safety. From an early age, teach him to wear a helmet and pads for his elbows and knees. Insist that he wear shoes. Crashing is a normal part of bike riding. Do what you can to protect him from serious injury. Above all, teach the rules of the road when it comes to cycling: how to signal, where to ride and, as he gets older, how to ride safely in traffic.

Family Outings   Bicycling is something you may want to do as a family. It's a great way to unwind together and to explore your city on an early Saturday morning. You may want to take your bicycles with you on family vacations.

40 ▲ Chores

It might be making the bed or changing the sheets on Saturday morning.

It might be cleaning out the bird cage or changing the puppy's water daily.

It might be dusting the furniture or pushing the vacuum sweeper in the hall once a week.

It might be mowing the lawn or raking leaves.

It might be scouring the bathtub.

It might be loading or unloading the dishwasher or setting the table for supper each night.

It might be emptying the wastepaper baskets.

Lots and lots of activities can qualify as chores. Chores are activities that are scheduled, assigned, and periodic (generally daily or weekly). And the scheduled assignee is 100 percent responsible for them.

It's Routine Doing chores should be part of kids' routines. Unless they are sick or out of town, they should be responsible for doing their chores without being asked and, generally speaking, without being compensated.

It's a Learning Experience   What do your kids gain by doing chores?

- They develop a sense of family responsibility.
- They learn personal discipline.
- They become aware of what it takes to create a clean, orderly, smooth-running home.
- They acquire housekeeping or yard maintenance skills.
- They learn that division of labor is the best way to get a major task accomplished, and that housekeeping or yard keeping work is not the sole or inherent responsibility of either Mom or Dad.

It's All in the Attitude   Insist that they do chores cheerfully and willingly. You'll be helping them gain a positive attitude that will carry them through a number of tedious and thankless tasks in life.

Periodically rotate chores so that children don't get stuck doing the same chore year after year.

And finally, insist that privileged activities—such as watching a favorite television program—cannot be pursued until chores are finished.

41 ▲ Map Making

Teach your children to read maps and to make maps. And then challenge them to map out their lives.

- Make a map of a room. Teach them how to measure and how to accurately record the sizes of objects.
- Make a map of your house or apartment. More measuring is involved. Your children may see home from a new perspective. If you live in an apartment complex, show them how the various apartments fit together to form a unit or floor.
- Make a map of your neighborhood. Locate key features. Introduce yourself to neighbors as you explain that your kids are making a map of your neighborhood and that you need to know how to label their house on the map.
- Make a map of your town. Obviously, a lot of details may be omitted. Ask your children to include the things significant to them.
- Make a map of school. They will feel comfortable starting a new school if you visit it

first and make a small map of it for them to study.

• Make a map of your church or synagogue. Teach the correct names of various parts of the building.

Take your children with you to your place of employment some Saturday afternoon or evening and let them make a map of your office or work area.

Accuracy   Map making encourages children to note details and distinguishing characteristics. The more your children mature, the greater the detail their maps should convey. A map also teaches them about directions, distances, and the need for accuracy in projects based on mathematical calculations.

Innovation   As your children write creatively, they may describe an imaginary town or island with stories about various characters who live there. The town could be set in another era and perhaps even in an imaginary country. Maps will help them clarify the make-believe community, city, or nation. Even stories about families are frequently written with a greater depth of detail if children first draw the floor plan of the make-believe family's home.

Route Finding   As you take family vacations, let your children take turns at being navigator. Teach them how to read road maps and how to map out a desired route. (They will ask far fewer "when will we get there?" questions.) If you have the privilege of traveling by plane with them, familiarize them with air route maps.

"You Are Here"   As you shop in malls, enter unfamiliar high-rise buildings or office complexes, or visit tourist attractions, consult the maps near entrances or elevators. Show your children how to get bearings in a strange place and which way to turn once they discover the "You Are Here" point on the map.

Global Perspective   Provide a globe. When you hear about events in the news, look up the locations of various nations and states.

Spatial Sense   Maps give kids a sense of "space" and of control over their environment. Television rarely depicts the real world in any spatial sequence. A program may readily hop from London to Los Angeles with one swift cut. Furthermore, television often depicts home settings that are far more spacious, with far more levels, than are typical of the homes of most viewers. The real world is a world of spatial reality. Put your kids in touch with it.

42 ▲ Church

Participate in a church regularly. Make attendance a part of your family's weekly routine. If your particular church doesn't have a program aimed at communicating with children, either start one or find a church that has one.

Children and the Faith   The following activities are suitable for children:

- Church-related social functions. These include annual picnics, after-church social hours, and children's outings and day camps.
- Programs designed especially for them. Children's speakers, clowns, balloon sculptors, puppeteers, and stunt skateboarders have been known to visit churches and synagogues to convey religious messages.
- Services in which missionaries speak or show slides or videotapes. Tales of faraway places always intrigue children.
- Musical programs, especially pageants that include costumed actors and actresses.

- Programs in which a well-known athlete is the guest speaker.

Youth Group Most denominations and most churches have a youth group. Encourage young people to participate fully. Go along occasionally as a sponsor or chaperone.

Many churches have youth choirs. Kids will learn about music and the church. And this group activity teaches social and interpersonal skills.

Some churches sponsor Scouting groups, have Bible study times (catechism training, vacation Bible schools, and so forth), or hold fairs and parties just for children. Point your kids to these non-TV opportunities for fun and fellowship within the context of faith.

Encourage your teenager to work in the church nursery or to teach a church school class for younger children. Help your teen study the lesson and prepare graphic displays and activities appropriate for the age of participants.

43 ▲ Listening

Earlier, we addressed the idea of establishing an atmosphere of peace and rest in your home. This chapter emphasizes the need for kids to develop listening skills—something they can't do with the TV blaring in the background.

Music Listen to music with your kids. Don't just have it on as background noise. Acquaint them with truly great compositions. With repeated exposure, they will anticipate certain musical phrases and passages.

Outdoors Listen to the sounds of the night together. Sit out on the porch, balcony, stoop, or deck, and take in the night sounds. They may be city sounds: sirens, honks, and other noises. If you live in the suburbs or in a rural area, listen for the insects; learn to identify them by the sounds they make. Listen to the wind in the trees.

From time to time, challenge your kids to sit near you and then to close their eyes and identify as many different sounds as they can. Make it a game. If you're in the park or other outdoor location, listen especially for the songs of birds. If you're in the zoo, close your eyes and listen to the sounds of various animals.

Other People In conversations with your kids, emphasize the need for developing good listening skills. They can't remember what you tell them to bring home from the corner market if they don't first listen to what you say. Quiz them —in an informal way—on what they remember from plays, sermons, or radio news reports.

Listening is a skill your kids will need all their lives. The better the skills, the better their chances of success at whatever careers or projects they undertake (including marriage!). Rather than "listen" to TV, encourage them to listen to life.

44 ▲ Letter Writing

Encourage each child to adopt a pen pal:

- A friend with whom letters are exchanged across the neighborhood
- A child in a foreign land
- A soldier
- A cousin who lives in a different city or state

Your child will develop language skills as well as a sense that the world really is a small place.

What to Write   Offer a few ideas about what to write: (1) friends, (2) family, (3) holiday customs, (4) sports, (5) favorite pastimes, (6) pets, (7) activities, (8) school, (9) books, and (10) goals in life. Encourage your child to ask questions, too.

Others to Write   In addition to ongoing correspondence with a pen pal, encourage your children to

- write letters of encouragement to friends who become sick or hospitalized.

- write letters to grandparents (or parents) who may live far away.
- write a thank-you letter for each present received.
- write to their member of Congress, senators, governor, state legislator, and to the president of the United States. Your children may tell the official that they are praying for him or her, that they appreciate the work that the person is doing for the good of our nation, and then close by asking a question or two. They may ask for a photograph of the leader.
- write to athletes, astronauts, and other people your children admire. They need only say, "I admire the work you do!"
- send postcards to friends while on vacation.

Your children will enjoy getting mail addressed exclusively and personally to them. To receive letters, however, one must also be willing to write them.

45 ▲ Room Cleaning

Children aren't born knowing how to clean. They must be taught how to vacuum, dust, clean windows, remove spots, and scrub bathroom surfaces. Children must be taught how to make a bed, hang up clothes, and pick up objects. And they can learn these skills at an early age, most effectively by working alongside you as you clean.

Orderly Living   Children aren't born with a well-developed sense of order. That, too, is learned. They aren't necessarily slobs or disobedient in having messy rooms. They may not see value in living in ordered rooms. To put rooms in order, however, they need sufficient space, shelving, pegs, hangers, baskets, stackable units, drawers, and so forth for the sorting and organizing process.

A desk for each school-aged child is recommended. That's the ideal place for doing homework, working on craft projects, and storing personal papers.

Once children have experienced living in an ordered world, they prefer it. They draw a sense of comfort from knowing where things are. They like the control of getting a toy, using it, and returning it. Children who are accustomed to being clean and living in clean surroundings are more comfortable with clean; it simply feels better to them.

Room Rules   You can insist that kids not eat in their rooms to reduce the potential for messiness and staining. You can require them to make their beds each day and to put dirty clothes into laundry hampers. You can also insist that they keep any pet cages cleaned out on a daily basis.

Organization   Teach them how to organize clothes and personal things, and how to set up files and binders for keeping things readily accessible. Boxes, baskets, and stackable units are helpful. Everything from magazines to underwear to paper clips can be separated and sorted. A certain amount of organization also saves time in getting ready for school or church.

Trash Days   From time to time, join your kids in deep cleaning. These trash-out, mattress-turning, moving-all-the-furniture-away-from-the-walls days are great times of discovery. Your kids will be delighted to find the missing "something" that slid through the cracks or got wedged where it didn't belong.

46 ▲ Decorating and Remodeling

Children can help you with decorating and re-modeling projects around your house or apartment, and they will be especially interested if those projects involve their rooms.

Teach your teenager how to make curtains, throw pillows, and perhaps a slipcover or bedspread.

Show your teen how to put up a shelf, paint the trim around the windows, and paint or wallpaper a wall (and perhaps add a wallpaper border).

Explore with your kids different ways to arrange their rooms. Ask them periodically to help you rearrange other areas of your home.

Fixing Up While Growing Up   Working around the house, puttering in the family workshop, and fixing things up are activities children should experience during growing-up years. Too often, however, parents are busy while children are immobile in front of the TV. Turn off the tube and invite their participation, even if the project takes longer. Count it a learning process for them as well as quality time spent together.

Family Projects   Projects that involve the entire family—such as clearing a patch of ground, relandscaping, or building a deck—add value to your piece of real estate and to your lives. Invite your kids to record handprints or footprints in the newly poured cement (under your supervision, of course).

Neighborhood Projects   If you live in an apartment complex or a suburban neighborhood, you may want to join with neighbors for a remodeling or upgrading of your entire neighborhood. Explore ways in which you can make your immediate neighborhood a more aesthetically pleasing area. Fix things that are broken. Sponsor a youth art contest and allow young artists to paint original works over the present graffiti. Plant a few trees or bushes (especially those of the low maintenance variety).

Share the work as evenly as possible. The more people join in the process of repair, the less damage is likely to occur in the weeks and months ahead. Above all, involve your children. Let them contribute both ideas and working hands. They'll have a sense of community involvement and accomplishment and, with that, a sense of community responsibility.

47 ▲ Gardening

Give your kids a plot of earth they can call their own.

- It might be a sandbox that becomes a "dirt box."
- It might be a windowsill garden box just outside the bedroom window.
- It might be several rows in the backyard that are turned into a family vegetable garden.
- It might be a designated flower bed.
- It might be a few small containers for growing herbs.
- It might be a large container on the balcony or deck.
- It might even be a small "greenhouse" kit.
- On the other hand, it might be an acre of the family farm.

A Learning Adventure   Let it be a place where your kids can

- plan what they want to grow and prepare the soil for that particular crop.

- plant a seed and watch it sprout and turn into a plant.
- learn about cultivation—the need of all growing things for water, nutrients (fertilizer), weeding, pruning, and a pest-free environment.
- learn to identify the parts of a plant and the various stages that a plant goes through in developing its fruit.
- learn when to pick ripe produce and, after harvest, how to clear the plot of earth and prepare it for the next crop.

Whether growing flowers or vegetables, herbs or cacti, your kids will learn more about the processes of life, the foods they eat, and themselves as tenders of the earth.

Furthermore, gardens require nearly daily care. Weeding, watering, and harvesting are activities that build a certain amount of discipline and consistency.

In this day when environmental issues are at the forefront of our thinking, what better way to teach your kids how to be caretakers of the earth than to give them a little bit of earth to take care of!

48 ▲ Homework

Right next to "clean your room" in the Groan Department is a parent's insistence that children "do homework."

A Priority Homework should always take priority over television viewing. In fact, it should be done first and done accurately . . . neatly . . . completely . . . and creatively . . . before the television set goes on. On most nights, that should just about preclude TV watching all together.

Don't let them take homework shortcuts to get to the TV set on time. Insist that they give best efforts to homework. Instill a desire in them to go beyond the assignment and to do something extra—to learn a bit more, try an extra problem, go for the extra credit assignment, study a little harder, or be as creative as possible in presenting the assignment. In the real world, that approach to work wins the promotion or launches a new company.

Putting homework as a priority before television not only ensures that homework will get done, but it

- sends a signal that you consider school to be the most important item on their agendas.
- compels your kids to engage in a version of time management.
- mirrors the real world—at least the world in which work must be done so the bills can be paid before play can be enjoyed fully.
- instills in them a habit of enjoying the processes of life (the homework) as much as the rewards (the desired TV show).
- establishes the idea that life inevitably has choices and that not everything they want to do in a day is always possible.

Don'ts and Do's   Don't nag your kids about homework. Expect it to be done as a matter of obedience.

Don't agree with them when they moan about having a lot of homework. Let them know you feel they are capable of accomplishing a great deal. "Just think. You'll be even smarter by morning!"

Do help with homework when they hit a snag. That does not mean you do the homework for them. Talk out the problems with them. Show them how to work a problem or research a topic or solve an equation or look up an answer. Periodically ask your kids to explain what their homework is all about. You'll gain new insights into the world that they face every day.

49 ▲ Creating Special Places

Children love to create and then spend time in special places all their own.

Outside and Inside   Work with them to create at least one outdoor and one indoor space primarily for their benefit. Outdoors, that might be a fort, a tree house, or a playhouse. A gazebo or a cleaned-out storage shed can be converted into or designated as a place just for play. Make certain that your kids can come and go from the place at will without danger.

Indoors, the secret place might be a converted closet, the space under a card table or dining table, or a large box turned on its side. The space need not be permanent—it can come and go as you and your kids desire—and it need not be fancy. A pup tent in a child's room may be an ideal permanent secret space to which she can retreat for moments of being "invisible" to the rest of the family. For the young child, a quilt on the floor or a playpen can be the designated private space—a convenient and portable one that can move from room to room as Mom or Dad goes about family chores.

"Worlds" of Their Own   In addition to child-sized spaces, kids can create "worlds" using blocks, Legos, Tinker Toys, and other construction sets. These worlds are occupied by dolls, paper dolls, miniature figurines, and imaginary friends. Toy trucks and cars roam freely on imaginary streets.

Your kids can build an entire city around a train set—positioning and repositioning buildings and designing new routes in and around table legs and under a corner of the bed.

They can occupy a hallway and turn it into a fun house filled with pillows and rubber balls and stuffed animals—a place to curl up on a rainy day and make up scary stories when the lights are turned off and the hallway is plunged into near total darkness.

Perhaps you have a basement or an attic with a small space for your older child's or teen's use. That can be just as valuable as adding another room to the house, especially if the teenager shares a bedroom with a younger sibling.

50 ▲ Group Lessons

Permit your kids to participate in a learning group of their own choosing apart from the formal school structure:

- A gymnastics class
- A ballet class
- A tap dancing class
- An art class
- An aerobics class
- A baton-twirling class
- A cheerleading class
- A drill team class
- A consumer-awareness class
- A self-defense class
- A cooking class
- A series of drama lessons offered in the neighborhood park
- A class that teaches good manners and social graces
- A choir
- A band
- An orchestra

Aims The group class may be aimed at helping children with physical conditioning, skills development, or psychological coping mechanisms.

The group class may be designed to help kids put an end to a destructive habit, provide skills and support for overcoming an addiction, or put to rest a hurtful experience. It may be a therapy group.

The group may be directly related to your church—a Bible study group, a personal evangelism training class, or another type of instructional class.

Group Interaction

Your kids will benefit from the interaction with others and the general atmosphere of give-and-take, questions and answers. They'll be comforted to know that other children start out just as uncoordinated, ill-equipped, uninformed, or emotionally bruised as they may be. They'll learn the therapeutic value of group process. They'll learn a new skill, generally at a less expensive price for the parents. And above all, they'll be participating in life rather than watching it go by.

51 ▲ Computer Work and Play

Your kids probably think that computer games are the next best thing to television. Indeed, on the distant horizon one can envision the day when computers and high-density television sets will allow for interchangeable software.

For now, you can rest assured that most of the skills they acquire by playing computer games are good ones. Eye-hand coordination, quickness in decision making, and a certain amount of reasoning skills are enhanced.

Problems The problems with computer games generally fall into two categories:

First, Children Frequently Are Allowed to Play the Games to the Exclusion of Other Activities If children are allowed to play computer games too much, they suffer the same problems as children who sit too close to a television set for too long. The eyes and bodies suffer strain, and the children become isolated from other people. The "play" on the computer is prescribed rather than child-created, just as with television. (The difference is that television is a completely passive activity, whereas computers involve interaction.)

Second, the Content of Some Games Is Undesirable   Many games are rooted in occult practices and use occult symbols and protocols for advancement by a player to higher and higher levels of play. Learn enough about a specific computer game to know if it is in line with the values you are trying to instill in your kids. Some games require violent killing or total wipeout of enemy forces—other values you may not want to reinforce.

Assets   Computer software extends far beyond games, of course, to top-quality educational programs. Among the most popular are "Where in the World Is Carmen Sandiego?"—an educational program that teaches world geography— and "Where in Time Is Carmen Sandiego?"—an educational program that promotes a knowledge of world history. The programs are loaded with content, require skillful reasoning, and are fun to work.

Texas Instruments has designed programs to strengthen math, spelling, and grammar skills. And most word processing programs are useful for teaching kids to type and write.

Children get a real kick out of manipulating art programs, such as MacPaint for the Macintosh line of Apple computers. They can create party invitations, illustrate stories, and prepare artwork to impress friends.

Computers are with us to stay. Just don't let them monopolize all your kids' time to the exclusion of other valuable play and learning activities.

52 ▲ Videos

Videos are the "television of choice."

The Good The good news about videos is that

- they are generally free of disruptive commercial messages.
- they can be stopped and started by the children, who retain some control, therefore, over the storytelling pace.
- they can be previewed by parents prior to viewing by children (and at hours that suit parents).

The Bad News The bad news is that many movies made for children today are laden with violence and occult messages—even those featuring popular cartoon characters. Monitor video choices closely. In fact, choose what your kids consume.

Most children enjoy a nonviolent video. They like action, to be sure, but they are just as concerned with characterization and a degree of fairness in the events portrayed. Not unlike adults, children like a good *story*. Children also enjoy a certain amount of long, slowly built suspense, something cartoons rarely attempt. Children like to see the good guys win and the bad guys punished. Children will often request permission to watch a good story again . . . and again . . . and again. Let them. They read and reread their favorite books. It's their way of learning a story.

The Guide   The *Family Video Guide* edited by John H. Evans rates eight hundred recommended videos according to entertainment value —from a poor rating of 1.0 to an excellent rating of 4.0. To be included in the book, the movie may not have an R rating and must have limited or no gratuitous violence, drug use, illicit sexual behavior, or excessive use of bad language.

The guide gives the year the film was released, a brief description of its content, the Motion Picture Association of America classification for the movie (for example, G, PG, PG-13), the age of the youngest person to whom the film would appeal, the running time of the film, and whether it is in color or black and white. It provides a description of any "bad language" (according to definitions for mild crude, moderate crude, vulgar, and profane). The guide may be ordered through Movie Morality Ministries, Inc., 1309 Seminole Drive, Richardson, Texas 75080-3736.

▲ A Final Word

Children *can* live without a steady diet of television.

The weaning process, however, may be tough. Start by limiting television use an hour a day until you are down to no more than four hours a week of nonnews programming.

Choose with great care what your kids will see during those hours. Let TV become just another activity in their lives—not the primary activity, the preferred mode of entertainment, or the major preoccupier of their thought lives.

You may need to spend additional time with them as they make the transition from a television addiction to a full-life experience. You may need to teach them—and perhaps yourself—how to play, how to explore, how to converse with others, how to find pleasure in quiet yet stimulating, active yet nonaggressive activities. Make the effort! Both you and your kids will benefit.

Phil Phillips is an author, commentator, and lecturer. As the director of Child Affects, a Christian nonprofit children's advocacy organization, he averages over two hundred speaking engagements each year.

To schedule Phil Phillips for interviews and speaking engagements, write to:

Child Affects
P.O. Box 68
Rockwall, TX 75087

Or call:

214-771-9839

Or fax:

214-722-1721